THE 10X AUTHOR

LEVEL UP OR BE LEFT BEHIND

SEAN M. PLATT

JOHNNY TRUANT

THE MATH OF MAKING IT

WHEN I WAS 23 years old, I thought math would save me.

I was working in a lab at the time, counting fruit flies in the name of science. It was miserable. The lab smelled like yeast because the flies lived on yeast paste. I had no friends in the building. My main social interaction was with a diminutive Asian woman who kept taking the grounds out of my personal coffeemaker so she could brew tea. Every time I went for coffee and found the carafe filled with tea, it gave my day purpose. I had earned an enemy but no allies. I didn't complain. One enemy was better than nothing.

Down the hall, a disease researcher kept mosquitos. I lived in fear that they'd escape and we'd all come down with malaria. Out of every three hours I should have been working, I spent two walking the endlessly connected hallways to find new paths through the complex. It's almost as if I didn't want to be there. Almost as if I'd have done anything other than keep working my shitty job.

Fortunately, I saw salvation in the form of compounding interest.

See, I was a fiction writer. I hadn't published anything, but I'd written plenty. This was the stone ages of publishing, and back then you still needed someone's permission to be an author. You needed to impress an agent, who'd impress an editor, who if you were very lucky might give you a chance to impress readers. I was okay with this because I knew that along the way to becoming the next Stephen King, I could write and sell short stories to magazines and literary journals. Only the best magazines paid well, but I figured I could make up for it in volume.

Instead of selling one project for $10,000, I could sell ten for $1000 over the course of an entire year. Or twenty, for $20,000 total. I was just out of college and my fiancée had a good job. I could live on twenty grand a year, easy.

That was my plan. I was going to write and

submit my work for sale. Then I'd do it again. And again.

And again and again.

Unfortunately, it turned out to be very hard for a newbie to sell fiction for $1000 a pop. Or $100 a pop. Even $10 took some begging. And forget about selling ten or twenty a year (let alone hundreds); even seasoned authors were lucky to offload more than a handful. But I was undaunted. I could *do* mass action. If I just found the right buyers, I figured I'd bury them with words. The only scenario I couldn't handle was one in which nobody bought anything, because zero times any number remains zero. But on the other hand, any *real* amount, no matter how small, could be multiplied. It was just a question of how hard I was willing to work.

My formula at the time went like this:

(Any non-zero amount of payment) x E = Success
where "E" is the amount of effort required.

AND SO THAT'S how I wrote back then: with gritted teeth, a chip on my shoulder, and a goal in mind. I kept telling myself, *Getting out of this job is just a matter of math.* If I could earn *something* (anything!) once, I could earn it over and over until I had enough to leave the fruit flies behind. Even a small number multiplied by infinite effort was *bound* to result in something.

That's how math was supposed to work, dammit.

Unfortunately, math failed me. I collected a lot of rejection slips but no paychecks for my fiction. I got nonfiction gigs and side-hustles, made my living that way, and eventually returned to storytelling ten years later when the Kindle was born.

Digital self-publishing was brand new then, and authors at the time were inspired by success stories like Amanda Hocking and John Locke, who sold their books for under a dollar but pumped out tales so fast their fingers had to hurt. Quality mattered … or maybe quality didn't matter at all. In his how-to book, John Locke said he wasn't exactly reaching for a Pulitzer. In fact, he said he didn't need to be *anywhere near* as talented as well-known authors. The reason? The Tom Clancys and Margaret Atwoods of the world were selling ebooks for ten dollars or more … but because *his* books only cost a buck, Locke reasoned he only had to be a tenth as good.

Quantity mattered a whole lot more than quality back around 2011 — seeing as all those brand-new Kindles people had bought needed enough books to fill them.

Ultimately, it came right back to math. Suddenly, to be a successful author, you didn't need permission. You needed bulk, timing, and luck. Hocking and Locke were only earning around thirty cents per book, but they'd proven that any non-zero amount of payment multiplied by effort equals success. *Big* success, in both of their cases.

Learning all of this put the spring back in my writing step. Authors out there were making a killing, thanks to the math that had eluded me. *Now* the formula actually worked. Hocking and Locke earned their tiny royalties *over and over and over again*. Write enough and sell enough, and even thirty cents adds up.

There was suddenly a light at the end of the tunnel.

But that was the Wild West, back when ebooks were new. I came into the biz at the end of that first wave, just as things were starting to change. My partners Sean and Dave had been riding the updraft, and I'd written myself a surfboard so I could ride it, too. I had a book; I was ready to cash in and make serious bank. I even knew the tricks, which I vowed to employ shamelessly. The one that worked best was simply changing your book's price to $0.00. You made it free, gave away a ton of copies, then changed the price back to a dollar or more. Your already-high free ranking converted to a paid ranking when you did that, and suddenly you were top of the charts, selling (for cash, this time) hand over fist.

Magic buttons? I could *do* magic buttons!

But of course, Amazon closed the loophole and the strategy stopped working. Authors freaked out. New loopholes opened and were quickly exploited. Amazon closed them again, and again, authors freaked out.

On and on it went, until 2018 hit and the author community started singing the blues — for real this time. The market had saturated, they said. Selling books had become way harder. There were too many authors writing too much stuff, along with a lot of scammers effectively working the system. All those Kindles that'd been empty and begging for content in John Locke's day were now overflowing. You couldn't *give* books away, often literally, and even if someone downloaded your work for free, they seldom slashed through the hoard to read it.

The loopholes stopped working. The romance

market ballooned, then went from overflowing with millionaire authors to so cutthroat that only a handful earned anything better than peanuts. Trends came and went. Authors chasing post-apocalyptic stories, vampire stories, LitRPG stories — all of which were hot for a minute, then overfilled, then cooled off.

Amazon introduced its Kindle Unlimited program, making a ton of money for well-positioned authors but devaluing books for a massive swath of the reading audience — those who decided that if a book wasn't included with their KU membership, they didn't want to buy it no matter how low the price.

The online bookstores saturated with poorly edited, sloppy stories. A flip-side of the "not having gatekeepers (or quality control) is a good thing" argument. That changed reader behavior and expectations, which altered the market again. Many readers became KU-allegiant and cheap. Others became so frustrated by the landslide of titles being sold by no-name writers they ran back to authors they already knew. Why take a chance on someone who's not a household name when so much of what was being published in the indie market was sloppy, ill-conceived, and sometimes scamming garbage?

As the sky fell in the late twenty-teens, many of the same indie authors who'd been so excited by digital self-publishing became a lot less interested.

What ... there's no easy money? What ... I can't expect a bestseller right away? What ... the fact that my book is online and my mom likes it won't guarantee sales?

What ... this requires hard work, patience, business acumen, and quality?

FUCK THAT!

A lot of authors started to bail. When word-smiths who'd built little empires started saying that the floor was falling out from under them. Not because the market had dried up per se, but because the whole "author thing" had stopped being easy.

But here's the important part. Here's what I want you to take from this little introductory essay.

The late twenty-teens, scary as they were, were also when the biggest opportunities appeared for writers with good heads on their shoulders who don't mind hard work.

Because you see, *today's author market is still all about math.* Only now, it's the math of 10X. (Pronounce it "ten X" and use it as a verb if you want to sound cool. Saying "ten times" is for poseurs.) You do the work, you do it abundantly and consistently, and you get paid. It's not as cheat-code, pushbutton easy as it used to be, but that just means the wimps are dropping out.

Soon, only the resolute and hardworking will remain.

And to them — to those serious authors who stick around and do good work — will go the spoils.

This all means one thing: *If you want to survive and thrive in today's game, you've got to level up, buttercup.* You need to 10X what you're already doing. That means becoming ten times smarter. Ten times better at what you do. You need to buckle down with ten times the focus, holding strong with ten times the grit.

If you aren't willing to do what it takes to 10X your author business (and to remember that it *is* a business, complete with sensible business rules), you'll perish as soon as you begin.

But the good news is that if you *are* willing to become a 10X author, you'll reap a lot more than ten times the reward. The sad truth is that very few people are willing to work as hard as it takes to realize their dreams, and that leaves room for others to realize them instead.

What about you? Are *you* afraid of a little hard work?

This isn't a nuts and bolts book. If you're looking

for the specific steps involved in publishing for a living, pick up *Write. Publish. Repeat.* or *The Fiction Formula*. If you'd like help with storycraft, we offer plenty of that in *Fiction Unboxed* and *The One With All the Writing Advice*. If you're into the details of how-to, check out Sterling & Stone's entire "Stone Table" line of books. There's plenty of specific tactical stuff in all of them.

This book is different. It's brief and to the point. It's practically a manifesto about what truly makes the difference. Its lesson is simpler than our larger, more in-the-weeds tomes ... even though "simple" is far from "easy." This book contains the advice that would help authors succeed most of all, but that few follow even if they understand it.

If you're the kind of reader who always needs a series of steps that goes *1-2-3*, what you're about to read will disappoint you. But I hope you don't stop. This is worth your time, even if there aren't any diagrams or engraved instructions.

Excluding those who "got lucky," what we'll tell you in the remainder of this volume is what makes the difference between successful authors and those who fail. *Period.*

I'll warn you: It's not sexy. You might even find it

boring ... although if you do, I'd wager you're not thinking hard enough.

There are no instant results in the world of the modern author. No gold rush. No sudden deluge of riches. If your career is anything like my crappy lab job, you almost certainly won't be able to quit to write full-time right away. But you *shouldn't* quit right away. Nothing you're about to read is about speed or being impulsive. It's about temperance, and moderation, and sense, and hard work.

Barf, right?

Well, maybe not, if it's what makes the difference between success and failure.

We won't waste much of your time. Not to spoil the punchline, but a large part of the formula is writing a lot. If you want to reach your author destination, you've got more important things to do than to read for one minute longer than is necessary to get the point.

So we'll be brief. The lesson, as we've already said, is simple.

Not easy, but simple.

Let's begin by talking about the saxophone.

DECIDING ISN'T ENOUGH

IT'S REALLY easy to decide to do stuff.

I remember being maybe ten years old, deciding I wanted to learn to play the saxophone. My dad was into jazz, and I thought it'd be really killer if I could just belt on the sax like the guys my dad listened to did. It was a sweet sound. Something to really bring the house down.

So my mom rented me a sax. I blew into the thing and it didn't sound anything like Dad's jazz men. I tried fingering different notes, but none of them sounded sweet. There even turned out to be one bonus key I hadn't known was there. You didn't press that magical key to make a note. You pressed it to drain spit from the bottom. Music was gross and hard. Nobody had ever told me that.

So after a few months, I gave up.

It had been so easy to get into the idea of sax-playing. Making the decision was where I'd felt all the fun, glamour, and potential. In the process of deciding, acquiring, anticipating, and preparing, I'd been happy. Life, in that particular realm, had been effortless.

How surprised and disappointed I was when reality descended! Turns out, the fun *deciding* part lasted only an hour or two. The much-less-fun, painful and boring, unsatisfying and hideously inept part of the process was practice — and *practice*, as I understood, could take days.

Weeks.

Years.

In fact, sometimes people who were great at the sax had been at it for *decades*.

I'm not sure you know this (it sure surprised 10-year-old me), but apparently very seldom does a sax player become great in a weekend.

This all sounds sarcastic now, but at the time I didn't really grasp that competence took hard work and practice. And it's not just my 10-year-old self who was fooled. Subconsciously, I thought things should be easier than they were for many more years — and still catch myself thinking it sometimes today.

I blame it on our society. This instant-gratification, push-of-a-button sort of world has trained us away from effort. If you've ever smacked yourself on the head and thought, *Well* of course *I suck! I'm still new at this!* as if it were a revelation, you're not alone. If you haven't ever done it, prepare yourself. You're probably still delusional, and if you're lucky, a reckoning is on its way.

Any skill worth building takes time. And not just time, but also a ton of relentless, sometimes-tedious and sometimes-agonizing *effort* that contains exactly no glamour. It's true of learning the saxophone. It's true of running distances, lifting weights, or losing pounds. It's true of playing video games and knitting and mixing music and painting and ballet. If you want to be good at something, you need to give it effort and consistency. (*See also:* Malcolm Gladwell and the Ten Thousand Hours rule.)

Now, we know what you're thinking, *Guys, I'm not stupid. I know that you have to practice to improve at something.*

If you truly understand that, you're in the minority. Most authors *don't.* They pretend say they do, but they don't. If they truly understood that time and effort and practice are all required for success, they wouldn't be surprised that flash-in-the-pan shortcuts don't work for long if they work at all. They wouldn't be disappointed when their first book sells just a few copies, or when it takes years of work before they ever see a nickel of profit. If authors truly grasped that you must work hard and be patient before you reap your reward, there wouldn't be an outcry every time some "ninja trick" stops working. If they understood, they'd get that if you put in the time and build your business right, you don't *ever* have to worry about the falling sky.

Even a falling sky can't make you forget how to wail on the sax.

Maybe you know some of the skills you need to write for a living. Maybe you know how to tell a good story, or use the publishing dashboards, or format a paperback. Maybe you think, because you know those things, that you've done your hard work and don't have shortcomings that still need practice.

You're wrong. I know because *I'm* wrong when I think that, and I've written over 100 books. My partners, who've written as much or more, know *they're* wrong when they start thinking they've practiced enough.

Remember, we're not talking here about your craft. We're not asking, "Have you spent enough time writing? Are you good enough at telling stories?"

No. What we're asking is, "Have you mastered the art of *running a writing business?*"

Again, if you say yes, I'm almost positive you're wrong. I know because we at Sterling & Stone are wrong when we think it, and our studio of a dozen-plus storytellers publishes multiple books every week.

You *can't* master the art of running a writing business, or any business. The best you can do is to become competent at it ... maybe even good. But you can't truly *master* it because the game keeps changing. The rules change; the market's appetites change; the finances of the whole thing change. It's a swirling bowl of constant flux, and your best bet is to simply try and hold on.

You need to put in more time, work, blood, sweat, and tears. You need to 10X yourself and your business. Learn, learn, learn. Try, try, try. There's incredible magic in the economy of what's required. It's simple. You just need to do it ... and that's hard.

I could keep talking in abstracts, but I think you get the point.

So let's talk about something more concrete — a metaphor we can all get our arms around.

And that's the metaphor of the flywheel.

THE FLYWHEEL

I'M GOING to blatantly steal a metaphor from Jim Collins's fantastic book *Good to Great,* which you should absolutely read if you're into business.

Collins's metaphor, which he gives for the workings of a great business, is that of a flywheel.

Imagine that in front of you is an enormous flywheel. It's mounted and perfectly balanced on a greased axle, free to turn. That last part, you have to take on faith. You've pushed on that heavy-ass thing to try it out, and it sure doesn't *feel* like it's moving anytime soon.

That flywheel, gentle writer, is your author business. If you push on it hard enough to get it moving a little, it'll throw off a few book sales.

If it spins at a bit faster, you'll get more sales.

If you can get it moving at high speed, your business will be trucking along well enough that you can live on your earnings.

Go faster than that, and you'll hit the bestseller charts and break the bank.

The problem is that the wheel is impossibly large, and *heavy*. You can press your shoulder against it and heave for hours and the damn thing will barely move. *How,* you wonder, *could anyone ever get it spinning at quit-my-job speeds?*

If you keep at it, though — if you continue to show up over and over for long periods of time and push on that seemingly-immovable flywheel, it'll slowly begin to rotate. You'll sweat. You'll feel discouraged and like what you're doing means nothing. Because the wheel takes all your effort and produces very little (or nothing at all), getting it started feels beyond thankless. You'll be sore, tired, and annoyed. You'll want to give up, because it's all pain and no gain.

The magic, though, is when Collins's flywheel finally begins to turn. It's so heavy that what used to frustrate you begins to work to your advantage — meaning that as hard as it was to start spinning, it's now equally hard to stop. You can go away from it a while and it'll spin with its own momentum. Subsequent pushes are easier, since it's already rolling. Because of this, each unit of effort you put into turning the wheel after it's already going gives you more and more results.

Basically, at this point the rich get richer.

We talked at the end of the first section about how the real difference-makers for authors are simple, but not necessarily easy. Spinning the flywheel is that exactly. It's hard to find a task simpler and more straightforward than pushing a wheel, but pushing it is far from easy. Only once it's really turning does its easiness improve, but by that time almost all authors have already quit.

This is too hard, they think. *It's not supposed to be this hard. I heard about XYZ author who hit the bestseller lists on his first try. I hear all these authors making six figures and more. I must be doing something wrong, because that's not the way things are working for me.*

Well, guess what?

You're *not* doing anything wrong.

This *isn't* too hard. It's supposed to be exactly this difficult.

XYZ author got lucky. People get hit by blimps, too, and you'd think that'd be impossible. Sometimes happy accidents happen. Some of those six-figure folks you keep hearing about got lucky, but most of them worked really hard in silence before finally getting to where they are. An "overnight success" is usually the result of tons of invisible effort — months or years of thankless, fruitless flywheel-pushing.

We hear the sexy stories on blogs and podcasts — who wants to hear an interview with someone who did the work every day and built her empire slowly?

So what's this got to do with 10X'ing your author career — and therefore your results?

With the Gold Rush days behind us and competition rising, lazy authors won't win. Neither will authors who figure they're doing "good enough." Even beating the next guy with better stories, characters, covers, and exposure isn't enough.

You need to 10X your game to stay in it.

But because you can't leap from zero to 10X overnight any more than I could master the sax before sundown, the real things you need to improve — the true skills you must achieve — begin in the mind.

WILL AND DESIRE

You know those arguments wherein Person A doesn't just want Person B to do something ... but also wants Person B to *WANT* to do it?

I don't want you to do the dishes. I want you to WANT *to do the dishes.*

I don't just want you to spend time with me. I want you to WANT *to spend time with me.*

They're impossible arguments. Agreeing to do something — even something you'd rather not do — is no big deal. You can do the dishes to keep the peace. You can do the dishes because leaving them dirty is gross. You can do the dishes because in a relationship, it's fair to share the duties. But if you don't already love doing the dishes, forcing yourself to *want* to do it for its own enjoyment is a tough sell. It's hard to talk someone into changing how they feel.

Unfortunately, all the successful writers we know could pose the exact same argument to all the not-yet-successful writers we know.

Don't just push the flywheel mindlessly day after day, even if all you do is tire yourself out and go numb from boredom — even if you don't see any results for month.

Instead, do all of that ... but also enjoy it.

Don't worry. It's not as paradoxical as it sounds. It basically means, "Keep reminding yourself how much you love writing." A weird little loop-de-loop happened when self-publishing started to take off, wherein people who loved writing for its own sake realized they could make money doing it ... then got all caught up in the *money* reasons and forgot that *love* started it all.

I'm no exception. Back in the days when I saw no future in fiction, I still made time to sit down and bang out words just because writing was awesome. It was my escape and could be super fun. It was thera-peutic for my soul. The fact that self-publishing became a lucrative business around 2010 should have been extraneous. I should never forget that even if Kindle hadn't taken off and fortunes hadn't beckoned, I'd have kept writing anyway.

In other words, don't try to write if you don't love the practice. Don't try to make your living as an author if you won't be happy until you're actually making your living as an author. Don't try to get rich quick from fiction if "fiction" is a lot less interesting to you than the "get rich quick" part.

Sean and I both have backgrounds in marketing. We've both been in mastermind rooms with very rich, very clever people who know how to make a lot of money fast. It would be easy for either of us to become millionaires within a year doing some sort of online marketing. We're writers because we love writing, end of sentence. There are far easier, far faster, and far more certain ways to make money if we didn't insist on writing as much as we can.

That's meant a lot of time with our faces pressed against the flywheel, trying to make it turn. The same goes for all the writers in our Story Studio, none of whom are bestsellers yet and all of whom continue to push their own flywheel alongside the studio's because the daily practice of writing is *what they love to do.*

Set aside your goals and career ambitions from time to time — and certainly during drafting hours, when you're composing fresh story. Don't work with iron willpower, gritting your teeth to get through something unpleasant so you can win your prize. Just like those frustrating arguments, you need to not just *do it* ... but *want* to do it, too.

Once you make that mental shift, everything gets a little easier. Even if you're paddling against a heavy current, you're at least enjoying the non-journey. That's good, because if you're like most working authors, you're going to be enjoying your non-journey for a while.

Maybe you've heard of Ernest Shackleton. In the early 1900s, he reportedly placed the following newspaper ad to find crewmen to accompany him to the treacherous South Pole:

Men wanted for hazardous journey
Small wages. Bitter cold.
Long months of complete darkness.
Constant danger. Safe return doubtful.
Honor and recognition in case of success.

Shackleton presented exactly the right message for those who enjoyed pushing the flywheel (in this case, the flywheel of arduous exploration), rather than appealing to those who were after a salary. If he'd played up income and glory and played down the negative stuff, he'd have had more applicants, sure ... but they'd have been the wrong type. A softer ad would have brought him men uninterested in the grinding thrill of the journey, suffering through it only to reach a payday at the end. And how would that have turned out, when their ship broke apart, when the risks turned to danger?

If we could write an ad to find writers to work with, it'd say this:

Writers wanted for unstable story studio
Small commissions. Disappointing sales.
Long months of labor with no end in sight.
Constant financial danger. Bestsellerdom doubtful.
Creative fulfillment and freedom in case of success.

Putting out an ad like the above would be absurd. That's why we did basically that when we were looking for our first round of internal storytellers. We sent a similar message to our email list. When a few authors responded, we reminded them how long it'd be before they saw a nickel with us.

Are you into lots of work and regular disappoint-

ment? Do you love writing and working with other writers enough that it, alone, will fulfill you ... because at first, there will be little else to drive you?

If they said yes and had some chops, we took them on. Some were better writers than others at the start, but skill matters a lot less than desire and determination. With time and effort, competent writers can become good writers and good writers can become great. Either, with practice and persistence and intelligent strategy, can build an audience and sell enough to pay the bills. Skills can be taught or earned through battle. It's attitude that can't be taught. Attitude — or at least the seed of a proper attitude — must be there at the beginning.

If you don't love the idea of pushing the flywheel without results for a long time (if you wouldn't sit down every day and write stories even if you knew you'd never make a penny) then you'll never win in this game.

If that's you, please stop trying to be a writer. Return this book and find another way to earn a living, so you aren't taking up space for those of us who love it.

But if you love the journey and not just the destination, there's great news: The hard work is handled, and all you need is time.

Well, time and some tools, which we'll talk about next.

THE 10X AUTHOR'S TOOLBOX

GRAB YOUR TOOLS

To write a good story, you need to understand structure and be able to shoot from the hip, or a bit of both. We assume you've got that much covered. Not perfectly, of course, because everyone can (and should) always improve — but good enough. You wouldn't have picked up a book on how to 10X what you're doing if you didn't already have something to 10X.

To sell books once you've finished them, you need to know how to format ebooks at least, print and/or audiobooks ideally. You need to know the basics of pricing, marketing, author branding, and funnels (wherein a cheap or free product "funnels" readers into buying more expensive products, or just *more* products). If you don't already know those things, you can learn them from our books *Write. Publish. Repeat.* or *The Fiction Formula,* from our Story Studio Podcast, or just from the Internet at large.

But to 10X yourself and your results in the way we suggest, the tools you need are far more powerful and far less sexy than any of that. By now, I hope we've set your expectations low on the sexiness scale. We're not talking about ninja tricks, block-buster promotional strategies, or even intriguing story twists that keep readers returning for more.

Nope. We're talking about things like hard work. Perseverance. Boring stuff that makes everyone roll their eyes, but that only truly successful authors do to the extent that's required.

The theme of this book says, "Be ten times more focused. Be ten times more resilient. Be ten times more dedicated to showing up every single day, putting in the hours and loving them, pushing that big, heavy flywheel."

But how can you do those things — how can you *make* yourself do those things? As we said at the outset, the "formula" is stupidly simple. But *easy?* Nope. It's hard to push that flywheel without fail, without losing faith.

So ... how?

The authors who succeed at 10Xing themselves in this way aren't superwomen and supermen. They've just trained themselves to endure and do what's needed, using the tools we'll tell you about in this chapter.

And those tools come down to installing a handful of beliefs in the recesses of your mind. Incorporating them is like turning your will into iron and adding armor to your thinking. Making your attitude Shackleton-grade resilient, to the point that a daunting journey simply becomes a daring adventure.

Teach yourself to believe what's below, and you'll find 10Xing becomes natural. Almost (dare we say it?) *easy*.

Let's start with a "meta" mental tool — one that will help you to use all the belief-tools that follow:

1

REFRAMING TURNS "HAVE TO" INTO "GET TO"

"REFRAMING," if you haven't heard of it, is the simple matter of taking something we tend to see one way, and amending it so we're able to see it another, more productive way.

For example, you can reframe *I have a stupidly long commute* into *I have so much time to learn new things*. If your commute involves someone else driving (a friend, public transportation) you can use the drive to read or take notes that expand your mind and skillset. If you drive yourself, you can listen to educational podcasts or audiobooks.

You can reframe *I have so much work to do on my business* into *I have so many opportunities to improve my business.*

You can reframe *My doctor says I have to lose*

weight for my health into *I get to explore so many new, active hobbies.*

Put simply, reframing is the act of turning *have to* into *get to.*

For me (Johnny), this is the master adjustment that rules them all. Like many people, I resist things I *have to* do. Tell me I have to do something, and almost for sure I won't do it, won't do it well, or will do it with a huge chip on my shoulder. Not the most productive way to shift the mind in the way necessary to become a 10X Author.

Maybe you've already begun a reframe as you've read this book. We've been trying to nudge you toward one. *Thanklessly turning the flywheel* sounds crappy when you first hear it. But hopefully you see that only the strong and bold have the fortitude to turn that thing day after day, and hopefully you like seeing yourself as strong.

If that's the case, you're already reframing the act of turning the flywheel from something you *must* do to something you *want* to do — not because you truly desire the act of turning it, but because you feel you're the kind of person who doesn't give up. Who isn't scared of doing the work.

Maybe you like the idea of yourself as "one of the few," rather than one more sheep following the herd.

You're a doer, the kind of person who acts on their dreams so they actually happen rather than waiting for a miracle to save you ... right?

If so, excellent reframe. Now, here's another reframe that will serve you well:

2

CHALLENGES ARE AWESOME

WHEN I WAS in my 30s, I was really active in an online weightlifting forum. There was this one guy — a Russian with all the fortitude and grit the West stereotypically associates with Russians — who kept posting videos of these extreme fitness challenges. The kind that made some people barf just watching, and that no sane person would want to go out and try.

I remember reading about one particularly bile-inducing challenge and replying to the others, "Yes, that looks hard as hell. But just think how tough you'd get if you did it!"

Not everyone shared my opinion about the challenge. You might not be a very athletic person yourself, and you might be reading this right now, thinking that crazy barfing workouts aren't tough at all. That's not the point. The point is that I looked at something unpleasant and said, "That's awesome *because* it's hard. The fact that it seems so hard is the *reason* it intrigues me."

Set aside the fitness connotations if they don't speak to you. Instead, consider anything you've read here that makes you itchy — something you agree you should probably do (like turning the flywheel without immediate results) but are less than excited about. Everyone's 10X challenges are different. Maybe you're realizing you need to get up earlier to write more before work, or maybe you just know you've got a long road ahead instead of the instant results hucksters like to promise when trying to separate you from your cash. Just pick something that sticks in your gut. Something you don't want to do, but know you should.

Now try some form of this reframe.

Doing difficult things isn't unpleasant. Challenges are actually awesome, because XYZ.

"XYZ" can be any reason you choose. Maybe you want to see yourself as the kind of person who never gives up, in which case challenges are awesome because they give you a chance to get through something that would cause quitters to quit.

Maybe XYZ speaks to your desire for freedom: *At work, I have to file TPS reports because the boss says to, but when I write, even if it's hard, it's something I'm choosing to do on my own.*

Maybe XYZ is about proving yourself to people who never believed in you. Maybe Mom or Dad or Granny thought you'd amount to nothing, but pushing that flywheel proves you're not nothing; you're a badass instead. (Sean has a little bit of that one. His career began when a high school guidance counselor told him he'd fall hard because he dropped out before graduation — and he's spent the past 25 years proving that counselor wrong.)

Turn *have to* into *get to.* Just reminding yourself that pushing the flywheel is something you're *choosing* to do already makes it 10X better.

3

PERFECT IS THE ENEMY OF DONE

GUESS WHAT? Perfection sucks. You can never be perfect, especially if we're talking about something subjective like writing books. In truth, the quest for perfection is almost always a delay tactic born out of fear or laziness. "I want it to be perfect" is something people say when they don't want anyone to hold them accountable. "It's not finished because it wasn't perfect" sure sounds like a lot better excuse than "I was afraid, or found something better on TV."

There is a genuine drive to improve, yes. Sometimes, the desire to make work better and better (or to learn more and more before acting) is noble. But often it's an excuse. When you insist on perfection, you never truly finish anything. You don't get it out into the world, for sale or consumption, so you can start on something else. Insisting on perfection short-circuits the process of shipping and moving on. Nothing goes out. You stagnate instead, working on the same dumb thing forever.

That's not pushing the flywheel. That's giving it a single half-hearted shove, then launching into tons of analysis about how hard you pushed it.

Stop analyzing so much. Stop insisting on getting every little thing right. Don't be afraid of making a few mistakes. Don't let fear of criticism (because you've published something "imperfect") stop you from publishing. Don't write the perfect book. *Just write the book.* Then put the damn thing out so you can write the next one, then the one after that.

Pushing the flywheel is never about naval-gazing and second-guessing past actions. Those things slow the flywheel, not accelerate it. Pushing the flywheel is about doing work that's good or great, never perfect.

Perfection is a terrible standard because it can't be achieved. Don't do perfectly. *Just do.*

4

GOOD ENOUGH ISN'T GOOD ENOUGH

OKAY, so this one appears to contradict what's above.

If "good enough" isn't good enough, doesn't that mean you should keep working until it *is* good enough ... maybe even *perfect?*

Nope, that's not what it means at all.

"Perfect is the enemy of done" and "Good enough isn't good enough" are both true — just on different levels.

On a project-by-project level of scale, you should ship when a book or project is as good as you can reasonably make it without obsessing. On a project level, you should never strive for perfection. Let your work be imperfect. Let your books have their flaws, so long as you're not being sloppy or lazy.

But then, when you begin the next project, vow

that it'll be a little better than the one that came before.

This year, strive to be better than last year. Maybe last year felt "good enough," but we're at the macro level now, ladies and gentlemen ... and on the macro level, you should always strive to improve.

As long as a quest for improvement doesn't become a paralyzing quest for perfection, it's a required ethic in your author life. That's because good enough *isn't* good enough in the big picture.

Good authors publish books and people read them.

Great authors have ravenous readers who will buy anything they produce.

Outstanding authors have 10X'd themselves, never settling and always striving for more. It's these folks who make it when even great authors struggle.

Now, when we say "good," "great," or "outstanding," we're not talking solely about the quality of their prose or storytelling chops. Those adjectives refer to the whole of a writer and their authorship business.

Outstanding authors are those who are always looking to write the best book description they can so readers will want to buy it. Outstanding authors are always working to up their book-cover game, either finding better designers or improving their existing relationship, always training and offering feedback and communicating their needs with understanding and compassion and generosity, so the end product improves.

The market isn't as sloppy and forgiving as it was in 2012. You can't put out *good enough* books and hope to survive. You can't get any old book cover from the cheapest designer you can find and justify it by saying, "Meh, it's good enough."

If you're saying that, trust us: It's not good enough.

One of the principles we live by at Sterling & Stone is paraphrased by the excellent book *Essentialism* by Greg Mckeown: "If it's not a hell yes, it's a no."

In the context of "good enough isn't good enough," this basically means that anyone who's not neck-deep in delusional thinking has an easy litmus to determine if you're on the right track.

Ask yourself, *Am I holding myself and my work to a high enough standard?*

If your response is lukewarm ("sort of," "maybe," "probably," or "I think so") then the real answer is no. You *know* it's a no because it's not hell yes. A believable answer should be emphatic. There's no doubt, when you're in the right place.

Is this book cover awesome enough to make potential readers want to buy?

Hell yes!

Have I pushed the flywheel enough recently?

Hell yeah, I have! I've got a full-time job and two kids and I still wrote two novels and five short stories this year!

There's nothing objective to the *hell yeah* test. It's an emotional thing. It's a gut-level feeling. You can puff up your chest with a HELL YEAH, BABY because you finally wrote your first novel even though it sucks and you're planning to throw it in the trash before writing a decent first novel, or you can say "hell yeah" to writing 30,000 words a week as a full-time author.

You can say "hell yeah, this is awesome!" about anything, as long as you feel it in your gut.

Just don't ever justify "sure" or "why not?" or the dreadful "meh" as an answer. Those aren't hell yeah, and that means they're no.

Which means they aren't good enough.

Which means try again, champ.

5

CONFRONT FACTS, BUT DON'T LOSE FAITH

A 10X AUTHOR is unflinching in the face of truth, yet never loses hope even if the truth sucks. It's a razor's edge, but walk it you must. Facing the truth can, at times, leave you mired in unpleasantness you're unable to deny. But at the same time, never losing faith can, taken to extremes, feel like soldiering on despite a whole lot of ... well ... *unpleasant truth* that seems to suggest there's no faith worth having.

Yet you must do both. Face facts with absolute self-honesty, while maintaining faith in your ultimate purpose.

If your books aren't selling, you can't stick your head in the sand, plaster on a happy smile, and pretend that all is well. Doing that is a sign of insanity or deep delusion. If you want to 10X yourself as an author, that means sharpening your truth-telling muscle to the point where you're able to face reality even when it's unpleasant. You might look at your catalogue and realize, *Oh, shit. These books are bad. These covers are terrible. My branding is so off-point, it's embarrassing. Forget about HELL YES. Everything I've done so far, if I'm honest, is a big old HELL NO.*

You might have quit your job to write, yet know in your gut that you leapt too soon — or that you jumped when times were good, but now the tide has turned. Maybe the economy shifted. Maybe your genre got a lot less popular. Maybe you got married or had a kid, and now need more money than you did as a free-flying solo. Maybe your spouse is nervous (as ours have often been) and you're honest enough to see (as we haven't always been) that in the name of domestic serenity, perhaps a more stable income is in order even if you really, really don't want a day job — or to stick with a gig you'd hoped to quit.

If that's the case, you must face what's true and do what must be done without fear, anger, or resentment.

But at the same time, you can't overreact. You mustn't let fear masquerade as truth or see something that might happen and convince yourself that it's true, in defiance of the faith you need in order to believe a statement as outrageous as "I can be a working author."

You must tell the truth, but must also keep the faith — which (let's face it) often looks like a whole lot of bullshit when held up to the mirror or truth.

This balancing act is hard to manage, and to learn. It requires practice through trial and error. Faith is a muscle, and your faith that *I can do this* or *I'm good enough to do this* or *I can make this work* will sometimes seem to clash with facts that might imply you *aren't* making this work or "dude, look at your bad reviews and pathetic sales. Clearly, you *aren't* good enough."

Worse, you may have faith ... but others may think you're using it to ignore truth instead of facing it. You might say, "It's working" while your spouse says, "Um, no it's not, because we can't make rent."

There's no easy answer to finding the line. It comes from experience, success, and failure. But keep looking, because doing both matters.

You must know when something isn't working, so you can fix what's broken.

But beneath it all, you must never lose the belief that you can make it work ... no matter how crazy friends and family may think you're behaving.

6

PROGRESS MATTERS MORE THAN PROFITS

THIS TOOL — this belief that all 10X authors need in order to succeed — is one of the hardest. We've certainly struggled with it. We've been tempted, over and over and over again.

The thing is, you need profit to survive. Very forward-thinking, security-minded authors may have squirreled away enough money to live for five years without earning a dime writing, but few authors plan that way. Most of us need our words to earn money sooner rather than later, even if only to justify the time-spend to ourselves or families.

But at the same time, profit often comes slow.

No, no; it's worse than that. *The choice that would lead to profit often directly contradicts what a smart 10X author would choose to do.*

So there's this struggle. You'll need your books to earn money, and you'll occasionally run into ways you can earn additional money. For example, you might learn that authors writing books in ABC genre are killing it right now, and decide to write a book in that genre yourself.

That's great, if two conditions are met:

1) You genuinely know, respect, understand, and personally enjoy ABC genre, and

2) The books you've written so far — and the author brand you've built so far — are compatible.

We know lots of people who started writing romance because romance was, for a while, where so many millions were being made. This despite the fact that they don't like or understand romance. One person in particular told us that she found her genre — and hence her readers — stupid. That's not a good way to live or earn a fan base.

We violated the second reason half a dozen times or more before learning our lesson. Chasing trends (vampire books are hot; biker romances are hot; LitRPG is hot) is tempting because of all the rabid readers, but every single time it's meant taking our eye off the ball.

Right now, Sterling & Stone is mostly about sci-fi and thrillers, so when we launched romances or

LitRPG novels, our readers were confused. They wanted to buy sci-fi from us, not romance. What's more, they no longer felt they could trust our sci-fi chops. We weren't releasing as much sci-fi (had to make room for all that other stuff), but the divergent books eroded our brand as a sci-fi engine.

They aren't sci-fi guys anymore, readers thought. *They're publishing all sorts of weird stuff now.*

In those cases — and many where authors chase immediate profits that aren't obviously in their sweet spots — it's a mistake. A diversion from what you're supposed to be doing, and ultimately slows progress toward your long-term goals.

Always choose long-term progress toward your ultimate vision or goals, even when it means taking the hard path and delaying profits today.

Although, while we're on the subject of author identity and branding, let's also turn to:

7

YOU ARE ONE THING, NOT ALL THINGS TO EVERYONE

THIS IS the *know thyself* section. Or more accurately, *know thyself, and ignore the temptation to be anything other than thyself.*

Want to know why releasing trend-chasing titles hurt our long-term forward progress as a company? It's because doing so confused our brand.

If you don't understand branding or need a refresher, the idea is actually super simple:

A brand is a promise that all of your interactions with the world, combined, make to your customer.

And:

The number one thing that maintains a strong brand is consistency.

Let's unpack that a little.

"Interactions with the public" consist of the

sights, sounds, feels, appearance, impressions, and discussion about you.

Your book covers are part of your brand. Your stories are part of your brand — the way they're told, but also the genre they're in, the way you tell them, the language you use in them, the jokes you make, the pop culture references you call on, and so on.

But your website is also part of your brand. How it looks, but also what you write there. If you ever meet readers in advance or email with them or interact with them on social media, all those things go into your brand as well.

For companies with brick-and-mortar offices, the person answering the phone, the decor in the lobby, and the attentiveness of the receptionist all go into brand, too.

Combined and averaged, all those individual things that comprise your brand make a promise to your customer — to your readers.

Your manner of writing, behavior in interviews, and the tone of your Twitter stream might promise readers a sweet old lady who traffics in cozy mysteries where nobody dies, or swears.

You might come off as dark and moody, promising thrillers full of threats worse than dying.

Turning to the second bit about brands, the way

you maintain yours is by being consistent. If you're that dark and moody thriller author, don't share a dust jacket photo of you wearing brightly colored clothing and smiling. Dark and moody authors should look and behave dark and moody. They should also write dark and moody thrillers, so writing a sweet romance just to shake things up or chase a trend will do something worse than *not work*. Because it's so inconsistent with your brand and breaks a promise your reader thought she could believe in (namely, that a book she buys from you will be dark and moody), the decision will hurt what's already working.

Chasing trends can easily move you backward.

The advice of this section is simple: *Decide who you are as an author and* be that, *consistently.*

This doesn't mean you must always write the same book on repeat. If you're careful and don't mind a much slower path to success, you could do what Sean and I did.

We *don't* stick to a single genre. We hop around constantly. But every book we write is intellectually curious. We ask big questions with our themes in all genres, then explore them. Use with caution, but it can be done — making something thematic part of your brand, rather than just your genre.

Choosing to be just one kind of author for one kind of reader, means you *won't* be the right author for a lot of *other* readers. Many people won't like your books at all, but *never change who you are as an author to please them*. Creating a brand, by definition, means you're only appealing to a small section of the population. Try and appeal to everyone, you'll end up strongly attracting no one. Instead, appeal as strongly as you can to your core and potential readers, even if that means ignoring everyone else.

OPTIMISM, PERSISTENCE, FAITH, AND OTHER UNSEXY VIRTUES THAT MAKE ALL THE DIFFERENCE

THIS LAST BIT in our toolbox chapter is the catch-all where we tossed all the little things that don't really warrant their own section, but that matter nonetheless.

In case this hasn't landed yet, every one of these tools is mental. You don't need to spend a cent to get them, or much time beyond practice. Simply decide to embrace and embody them. It doesn't take cash to reframe challenges as things that excite you. You don't have to book an appointment then spend a week in a classroom to decide that progress matters more than short-term profits.

There's really only so much to *do* if you want to 10X yourself as an author. You need to write well, yes. You need to format books, publish, sell, and keep learning. But we're assuming all of that. That stuff is a given. Your main job — your only real job, as far as we and this book are concerned — is to keep pushing the flywheel.

Everything we've discussed in this chapter is stuff that will help you turn the flywheel. It's meant to hearten you when pushing becomes hard. It's meant to give all of your endless effort some meaning, because otherwise it seems to have none.

All these tools, dear reader, are meant only to flip switches inside your mind — to make it easier and more fun to show up every day and do the work.

We've already talked about faith. Faith means standing tall and believing, even when things go awry, that you are doing the right thing and can make it all work.

But optimism, too, is invaluable. It goes hand-in-hand with faith. If you always see the bright side, it's easy to believe in the big picture. But optimism isn't just blind smiling. We joke with our third partner Dave because he thinks optimism is for suckers. Then he wonders why other people seem to get all the breaks.

Duh, Dave — they get the breaks because they're

optimists, which means they're always on the lookout for those breaks.

Pessimists don't bother looking, so they don't find opportunities. Optimism, my friends, is practical, not delusional. It's not pasting a smiley-face sticker on bad news. It's looking at all news, then finding a silver lining that could, if nurtured, get things on the right track.

And lastly, persistence. But do we even need to talk about persistence? That's what this whole book is about. Persistence is turning the flywheel day after day, week after week. Persistence is, simply put, never giving up.

It goes with faith, because it's simple to never give up if you have faith that things will work out.

Which all goes with optimism, because it's easy to see the silver lining if you have faith that it's all for the best in the end ... and if you know that tomorrow, you'll be pushing the flywheel no matter what.

We'll close this chapter with a warning: It's very easy to dismiss all of this as wishy-washy. *Where are the cool ninja tricks to bestsellerdom?* you might ask. *Where are the shortcuts that will let me earn enough to quit my job?*

And our answer, again, is *There are none.* Not any

that work consistently. The only thing that works is a commitment to 10X all you're doing. To put in the work with the right attitude.

Wishy-washy? No way. This, folks, is simply how it's done.

WHAT NOW?

Now you do the work. Period.

It's kind of balls. We get it. We told you this book would be short, that it'd tell you what actually makes the difference today for successful authors, and that what we'd tell you in these pages would be just about the least sexy success formula you've ever had.

Sorry to disappoint if that sounds discouraging, boring, or anything else. The real things in life are seldom rockets and fireworks. We could, in closing, pull out one final trick that you could start using to increase your sales by 20%. Sorry, but that trick doesn't exist. Or rather, it does ... but only you, in your unique shoes and with your unique understanding of yourself and your author business, can find out what it is.

What a rip-off.

And yet, the payoff is huge. If you believe what we've said here (and you should, because as unglamorous as it is, we promise it's the truth), then you know you're probably already doing the right things.

That's great news, isn't it? So many authors come to us frustrated, saying they've written books that people love but can't quit their stupid job on the stupid low income. They expect us to tell them how to fix it.

But friend, if you're truly writing good books that your readers love, you're not broken. You may have things to tweak (get that author brand shored up, maybe) or things to learn (our other books or free podcast archives will help with that), but the core of what's required is already in-hand.

You write.

You publish.

You repeat.

You push the flywheel, as long and as steady as you can. What other authors are doing well, you just need to 10X your mind to approach 10X better, with 10X more belief and fortitude and tenacity. You just need to be 10X more consistent, 10X more focused, 10X less willing to give up when the going gets tough.

Right now, I'm writing to you from the comfortable chair in my living room in Austin, Texas. I used to live in Ohio, but I wanted to be here. Writing let me do it. Sean, the co-author of this book and most of what I write, lives 10 minutes down the street. We have a bunch of great writers we meet with a few times a week, trying to build a world-changing company (a massive flywheel for all of us to push) together.

Our time is our own. We don't go into "real jobs" and we can, increasingly, do whatever we'd like. And we laugh *a lot*.

This great life didn't happen overnight. There have been dizzying ups and some terrifying downs. We've been on financial fumes more times than I can count. We've had conflict, both within leadership and with co-workers and partners. We've fielded near-disasters. Piloted programs that lost far more money than they earned.

It's been rocky, to be sure ... and even though I feel like I'm already living the dream, the struggle isn't over yet. Likely, it never will be. Once this flywheel starts to hum without fresh effort, we'll turn some of the work we'd been pouring into it toward something bigger. A larger flywheel, further up the chain. Making movies, maybe. Or video games. International bestsellers that everyone knows and enough leverage to change the world in ways we want, with story ... perhaps.

Despite changes in the indie book market, there's still a lot of gold-rush thinking. We hear about author superstars who hit #1 on the *New York Times* list out of the gate, or hear about six-figure launches from authors with no experience. It happens, sure. But those are the standouts. Those folks are the lucky weirdoes. For most of us, the rise to fame is seldom so rapid and stratospheric. For most of us, it's instead a slow and steady climb. More tortoise than hare.

In the end, slow and steady always wins. Work and perseverance always beat quick-fire tactics.

Just thought you should know, before you get your nose back against that flywheel.

And now, prosperous author ... *push*.

ACCESS THE VAULT

The best way to retain what you just learned is through reminders and application.

We've created a **60-Second Summary** of the key points in this book for you to print and keep handy as you begin to incorporate what you learned.

You'll find the summary, PLUS *all our extra downloadables for the entire Stone Tablet range* in our Extras Vault.

Visit **SterlingAndStone.net/Extras** to get access.